8.00

DISCARD

Memories
of Sweet Grass

Memories of Sweet Grass

Adelphena Logan

"The drum is a very personal item in the life of an Iroquois Indian ..... The drum sets a tempo for memories .....Memories of sweet grass ..... My drum is a mingling of past, present, future ..... A treasured diary of my people is measured in the beat of my drum."

Memories of Sweet Grass. Text and most craft illustrations by Adelphena Logan. © 1979 by the American Indian Archaeological Institute. All rights reserved.

Library of Congress Catalog Number: 79-65401

ISBN Number: 0-89488-006-3

The publication of **Memories of Sweet Grass** was made possible by a grant from **Reader's Digest**, and all proceeds from the sale of this book will be placed in a permanent endowment fund to assist in financing future publications of the Institute.

11741
Published by the
**AMERICAN
INDIAN
ARCHAEOLOGICAL
INSTITUTE, INC.**
Washington, Connecticut.

We, the editors, have accepted the task of bringing Adelphena Logan's **Memories of Sweet Grass** to publication. Although we were working only from her typed manuscript, we feel we have been able to maintain the flavor of her words.

SHIVER MOUNTAIN PRESS
Washington Depot, Connecticut 06794

 INDIAN PRAYER
FOR
DEL LOGAN

Earth Woman with hands
That shape the bread of time.
Earth Woman with
Pumpkin seed earrings and
Bracelets of wild plums.
Your house is made of summer.
Your children are the crops
Of all good seasons
Growing strong
In the house of the Earth Woman
Who weaves the thread of life.

And we were **all** "her" children!

Source Unknown

DEDICATED TO DEL

To Adelphena Logan
To our Del
    Dearest friend and wise counselor of my family
    Matriarch to our Institute
    Majestic in her strength, the epitome of
        Iroquois womanhood
    Her roots deep in her mother earth, straight and
        and solid as the taproot of the oak
    Her spirit strong as the hickory, mighty in
        her sense of outrage at injustice, infinite
        in her love
    Her hands supple as the willow, always creating
        something of pleasure, of meaning and of
        inspiration for the children of the world and
        all those who truly wished to learn
    Eloquent spokeswoman for her race and her beliefs
    A prophet from the past, to guide the present, to
        preserve the future
    A voice to whom modern man must stop and listen
        My teacher

Ned Swigart

    —A cabin in the wilderness
        August 12, 1978

DEDICATED TO PAUL

My good friend who likes to read, hear stories of the past, loves nature. He also proved what my people have always believed, that there is never any generation gap.

Paul fished and I sat and watched him. He shot at his target with his bow and arrow.

He brought me a chair to sit on each time I needed one. On my good days I would find my own place to sit and watch him. But never did we feel that I was too old or he was too young, even though we are sixty years apart.

We always said "thank you" when we finished our day.

Sincerely,

Dee

Washington, Connecticut
1977

CONTENTS

The Power of the Word - the Oral Tradition........... 11
Introduction...12
Drums...17
Corn.. 23
Iroquois Cornhusk Doll......................................27
Broom... 32
Pipes...35
Bark Crafts...39
Rattles...44
Cradleboard...48
Costumes of the Iroquois People........................ 52
Iroquois Basket Cap...58
Masks... 60
Adelphena Logan...73
Onondaga Prayer... 77
AIAI Acknowledgements.................................. 79

The Power of the Word - The Oral Tradition

When we were young it was our grandmother who gathered us around to tell us of many things: of how the world began; of where we came from; why we must respect all living things; of the wonders of the universe. She always told us of the old ways. And when we were told these things, these truths, we searched her face of many wrinkles and believed she must have been there, way back then, in the beginning -- so vivid were her words and the pictures she created in our mind's eye. It was only when we were much older that we realized that this was the way of the elders. Their words were the traditions being passed down from their grandmothers and grandfathers.

What is remembered is the influence of grandmother's words and the way these words guided our lives. We didn't know what we have come to know now; that in the beginning there was nothing -- nothing but the Word, and it was all-powerful. It is life itself. And the Word breathed life into Man. To the native peoples of North America the thought and the word were sacred and all-powerful, and from the Word there developed an oral tradition to carry forth and sustain life. It began the cycle of life and from this evolved our ceremonies to sustain our close relationship with the environment and to maintain the balance and harmony of the universe. The hypnotic quality of grandmother's carefully selected words healed us, cured us, strengthened and enriched our lives - which we were committed to pass on.

Trudie Ray Lamb
Director of the Native American Studies Program
American Indian Archaeological Institute

INTRODUCTION

We at the American Indian Archaeological Institute (AIAI) publish this book with deepest love and admiration and a profound sense of humility and grief at the passing, on July 31, 1978, of a great person who has touched and changed the lives of all who knew her.

We publish this book in memory of Miss Adelphena Logan, a direct descendent of the famous Telegua, Cayuga chief of the Iroquois.

I first met Del in the summer of 1971. It was one of those incredibly fortuitous accidents that happens to an individual during his lifetime. It changed the course of my and my family's lives and, as others were privileged to meet and work with Del, the entire fabric of our Institute. While my family and I were on vacation in the Adirondacks in north central New York, I traveled to the Owasco Restored Indian Village and Museum at Auburn, New York. As we were at that time contemplating the reconstruction of Indian dwellings for each ecological time period represented by our Indian Habitats Trail when we could verify the appropriate building plans archaeologically, I struck up a conversation with the only person I saw in the village—a dignified but very quiet woman who was setting up a craft booth. It was Del. A rare bond of friendship, affection, trust and respect was formed that day between us—two people of extraordinarily different backgrounds. This relationship was to flourish and grow as the years passed.

I asked Del at our first meeting if she would come down to speak to the newly incorporated Shepaug Valley Archaeological Society that coming fall. She did, giving an inspirational talk on Indian life and crafts before over 200 people in the Washington Town Hall. After this happy beginning Del was a regular visitor to our home and to the AIAI and attended most of our organization's important meetings.

On September 29, 1973, she and a number of her Onondaga friends from Nedrow, New York, to help us in our newly launched efforts to raise money to build a research and education center, prepared a traditional Harvest Dinner for over 200 people, and afterward shared with us traditional chants and dances. All proceeds from this dinner were donated to our American Indian Archaeological Institute Fund by Del and her people, a most precious gift. We successfully completed our fund-raising efforts to build this unique resource center dedicated to the discovery, preservation and interpretation of New England Indian history in December of 1973. In May, 1974, Del, with a number of New England Indian people, participated in our groundbreaking ceremonies; she opened the ceremony with a traditional prayer, which appears at the end of this book and which Del later used at all of our public meetings, including our dedication ceremony on July 1, 1975, when our Visitor Center officially opened. Del also assisted in removing the first symbolic shovelful of earth together with Irving Harris, Delegate-Chief of our local Schaghticoke Tribe. The tone of future celebrations was set when Del organized our first Founders' Day of craft and dance demonstrations in August of 1976.

Whenever we needed her expert wisdom and for whatever purpose, Del would make the long trip from Syracuse, taking valuable time off from her many other responsibilities. In the fall of 1976 we needed guidance in building an authentic reconstructed Indian longhouse in our new classroom. Del came down for two weeks, and with the help of our staff and local school children from four area towns, not only built the dwelling to actual postmold specifications, but also took it upon herself to find, donate or make most of the typical furnishings of such a dwelling.

True to her Indian tradition and as a symbol of her love and respect for our cause, she gave the AIAI many of her most precious belongings: her family cradleboard with designs on the back representing generations of the Logan family; a portion of a purple wampum string, symbolic of the last Logan chief of the Iroquois; and her wooden family utensils and containers, many given to her by her mother, to name only a few examples.

And so our years together passed, a lifetime of sharing in only seven special years. At the news of her passing, we were all deeply touched, not just by our own personal loss, but by the loss to all mankind, because Del cared so much and was willing to share so much of her exceptional life and heritage.

One memory of Del stands out beyond all the others—a picture of Del, weary from a long drive and all the pressures of her world, taking the time to show my eight-year-old son, Paul, how to shoot a bow and arrow she had made for him—standing, and then sitting on a small folding chair when she was too weary to stand—with infinite patience and love, always gently teaching.

And it is to Paul to whom Del dedicated this book, in a fitting tribute to her great love for children and her very special concern for one small, wide-eyed, eager boy. This dedication was made when, as if guided by

Drums

The drum is a very personal item in the life of an Iroquois Indian. It seems everyone in every family, somehow, someway has inherited a drum. For each it is like a book, a part of one's daily life. The drum sets a tempo for memories. It is a medium of release for our emotions. If we have sadness we use the drum as an outlet and we find solace. In anger there is relief and, if afraid, there is courage.

A drum reminds us of our lives. My drum is old and full of memories, memories of things learned long ago, of my ancestors and of the ideas and accomplishments of my people and myself. Memories of sweet grass, the closeness of nature, the ancient and beautiful things of the woods. My drum is full of voices... of paddlers and their canoes... of lone people going through the trackless wilderness... of the far, far voices of singers... of dancers—their feathers keeping time with the beat. My drum speaks of olden times, for it is a diary of my people. It tells of brave and solemn chiefs seated around council fires; of powerful bodies representing strength, endurance, stamina; of lofty spirits full of dreams, dreams of childhood and of the future. My drum is a mingling of past, present, future. A treasured diary of my people is measured in the beat of my drum.

WATER DRUM

The water drum was the only drum used by the Iroquois, and the Iroquois are the only people who used the water drum. We used this type because our songs have definite words. We sing words of our feelings and do not want just one monotonous note. By using the water drum we can pitch the instrument to the individual voice. A high voice requires little water in the drum, a deeper voice requires more water. Our singing, so tuned, is more pleasant to hear.

Drums can be made from various kinds of wood—basswood, ash, willow. Willow is the best because it is used to living in wetness; its fiber best retains the water. Because of its nature, the willow can be saturated with water over a prolonged period without side effects.

We walk through the woods looking for a willow that has started to decay. We take off a piece and char the inner portion. This makes gouging out the center core much easier. The piece should be tapered, about six inches in diameter at the top, at least five inches in height and about five inches in diameter across the bottom.

Hollow the drum so that it is thin as a shell, leaving about two inches of solid wood for the bottom. This bottom has to withstand the water, the drying out and the swelling that goes with the storing and the using of the drum. This leaves about five and a half inches of depth to be hollow space for the water. About three-fourths of the way up from the bottom make a small hole and a plug for it. This will be the hole used to fill and dump the water.

Make a ring or hoop of hickory which can be fitted to the top of the drum to hold the hide top in place. Slide the hoop from the bottom to the top, making sure it wedges firmly against the top of the drum. Calfskin is used for the top of the drum. This material tends to retain moisture so that it dries out slowly, can be reused without splitting and can take a lot of punishment as far as pounding is concerned. When the drum is taken apart, dry the calfskin carefully. When you wish to use the drum, soak the hide until it is saturated and pliable, then reassemble the drum. Always take the drum apart when it will not be used for a while. Before using it again, soak the skin top and the bottom of the drum until they are saturated.

The design on your drum can be painted according to what you want on it. Iroquois people put a small border design on the bottom. Sometimes they put no designs on at all, preferring to let the drum mellow with use and age. In the old days they would get hemlock pitch, coat the drum with it and then plunge the drum in boiling water. The water would dissolve the pitch, leaving the drum a tannish yellow. In addition to "painting" the drum, the pitch would seep into the debarked surface, plugging up all the little holes in the wood, thus sealing it and making it more watertight. When your drum is ready to be assembled, add the amount of water needed to tone the drum to your voice.

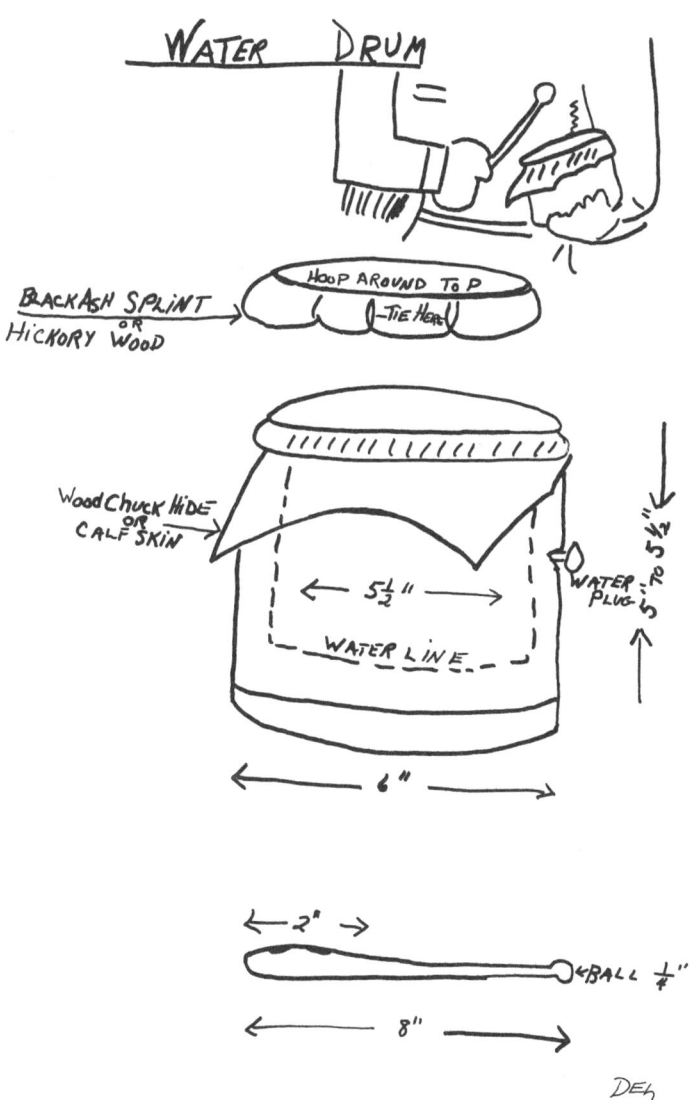

Corn

O - ne - ha

Corn was the greatest gift of the Creator to the American Indian. The knowledge of corn as a crop, which not only provided daily food but could also be stockpiled for the future, meant independence from hunting and resulted in the establishment of more permanent communities. Among the agriculturalists of the Eastern Woodland Indians corn became, in life and legend, THE life sustainer.

Early settlers would have starved if the Indian had not shared his corn. Indians also taught the colonists how to plant, harvest and use this greatest of gifts. As the settlers intruded on Indian villages they frequently burned the cornfields and granaries in an attempt to break the back of the Iroquois civilization.

Today the Iroquois communities are thankful for corn. Though their acreage has been reduced, they still remember to use the corn wisely and in its entirety. The kernel fed them; the husk, cob and stalk provided more comfortable living. So grateful were and are the Iroquois for corn as a part of their life circle that it is the only food used in the religious ceremonies.

Some usages of the corn plant:

Cob: Stoppers for jugs

"Cigarette lighters" — The Iroquois hollowed out a section of the cob, keeping a portion of this for a stopper. They placed a small coal in the hollowed-out section and replaced the stopper. Carrying this with them from place to place they could readily start a fire. Removing the stopper, they gently blew on the charred interior of the cob. Exposed to air, the cob flamed and acted as an instant fire starter.

Husks:

Thermos insulation — Husks were finely braided and wrapped around pottery pieces. For cold containers jugs wrapped with husks were placed in springs. When chilled the jug was filled, then stoppered with a corncob. Evaporation of water from the husk kept the contents cool.

Hot substances were poured into heated pottery vessels wrapped with braided husks. Stoppered by a corncob, the contents retained their heat.

Insulation for leather moccasins — Braided cornhusks were woven into a slipper shape. These were placed inside the leather moccasin and acted as a "thermal sock."

Mats — Coarse braids of husks were coiled with the husk tips sticking up rather than being woven in or cut off. When trimmed a nap-like surface remains.

Mattresses — Basically the same construction as the mat.

Baskets — The husks were braided so they could be coiled. Wetting the braids, the material was coiled into the size and shape of basket needed for a particular task. The coils were tied in place with sinew.

Burden straps — Husks were braided into the necessary lengths of straps needed to carry the burden.

Dolls — Originally the cornhusk dolls were not dressed. Neither were, nor are, faces put on them. It is felt that only the Creator may make a character, and character is revealed in the face. The details of cornhusk doll-making follow.

Masks — The Iroquois wore cornhusk masks in the Midyear Ceremonials. (The craft was made by the women. The husks were blessed.) They designated the workers of the services; in Onondaga there were thirty men. The wearers were sometimes doorkeepers, carried out the details of the services, notified the people who were to bring babies for naming, blessed and used the water in the naming rite and listed the names of the sick.

CORN HUSK MASK

ADDING HUSK

BRAIDED HUSKS IN SPIRALS TO MAKE SECTIONS

SEW HUSK WHEN BRAIDED IN SPIRAL SECTION

CORN COB SHAPING FOR NOSE

SPIRALS FOR BRAIDS

Iroquois Cornhusk Doll

In making the doll the cornhusks are first soaked in water to make them pliable (A). Several good husks are bunched and a knot tied in the middle as shown in (B). The upper sections of the husks are then pulled down tightly over the knot and tied into place around the neck (C). To further enlarge the head, several more husks are tied in the middle and placed over the partly-finished head (D) and (E). The upper sections are pulled down smooth and tight over the head and bound into place as before with a small husk. This completes the head of the doll (F).

After the head is completed, the arms of the doll are made by tightly rolling several selected husks (G) into a cylinder form (H). Dividing the ends of the husks that hang down from the head (I), the cylinder is placed between, the head is tightly bound to the arms. It is always best to tie the husks as tightly as possible, since they shrink as they dry.

Building up the shoulders is the next stage in the cornhusk doll construction. Several selected husks are bound on the shoulders and crossed over the chest and back of the doll (J). The kind of shoulders the doll has depends entirely upon the number of husks used. A real husky "fullback" can be made by wrapping a greater number of husks about the shoulders and binding them into place under the doll's arms (K).

The head, arms and shoulders of the doll are now finished, and it is ready for legs. Several cornhusks are wrapped about the waist of the doll and tied tightly. A broad husk is now wrapped about the waist of the doll, covering the ends of the husks just added. This band is tied into place with narrow husk cords at the top and bottom (L).

The legs are made by taking husks projecting below the waist and dividing them into two equal parts. In forming the feet, the legs are bent up and then tied into position (M). The arms are then bent down alongside the body and tied. This binding remains until the husks are dried, and the arms stay in that position.

Skirts for a girl can be made from broad husks and binding them about the waist (N).

Faces were never painted on these dolls since that was thought to give them life.

Although it is not difficult to make a husk doll, it nevertheless requires careful work and strict attention to directions, which is good training for everyone.

Cornhusks are saved on many reservations and the ears of corn are braided by means of their husks into long golden ropes and hung inside and outside of the cabins, a common sight even today.

Husk Doll

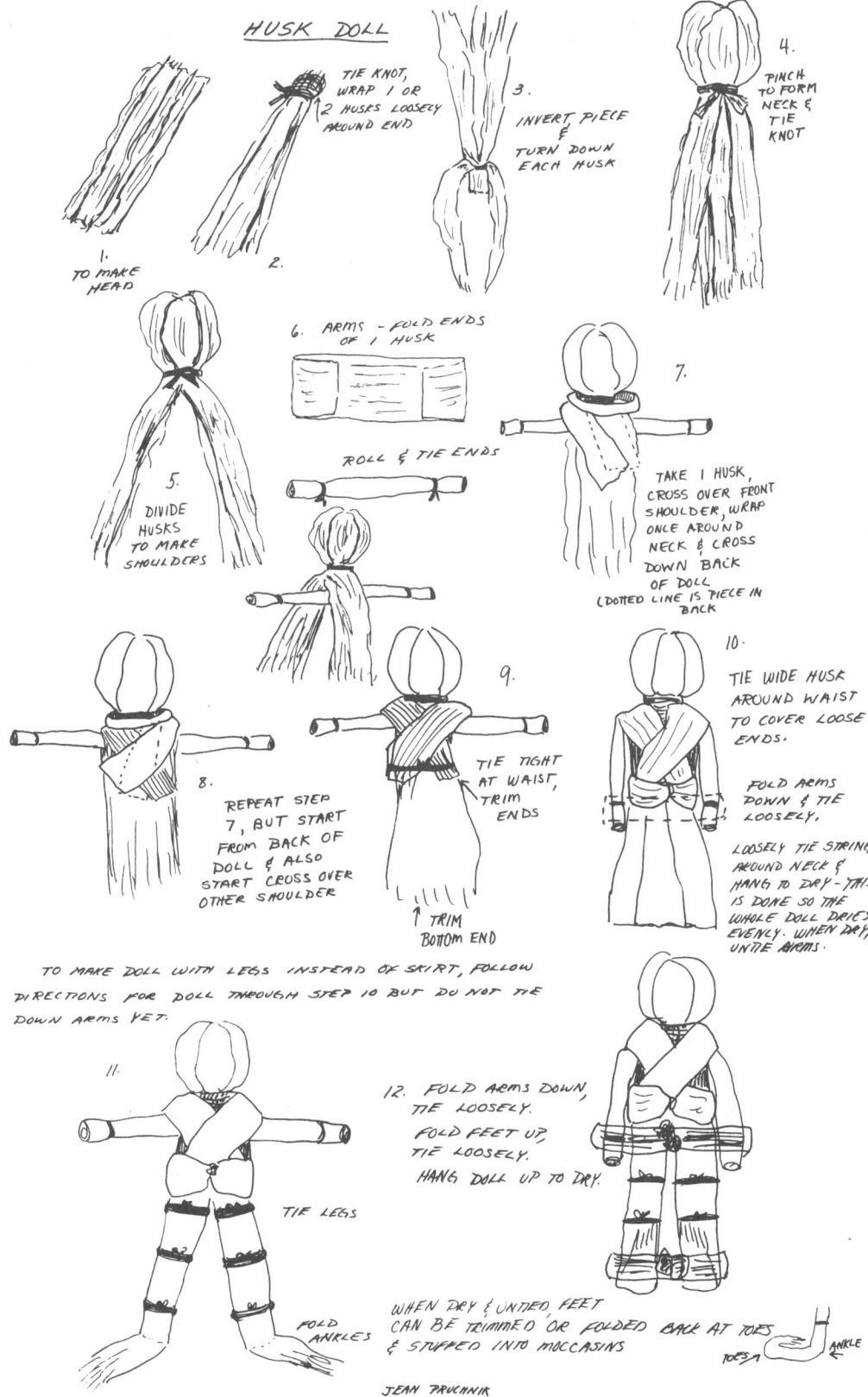

Broom

As many years as I can remember, our people have always had a handy broom made from black ash splints. It was made from a stick of black ash wood - just enough for a handle - and the splints of the ash wood, split, which were the bottom part.

1) The stick was soaked in water overnight, so that the splint of the ash wood would be damp when another stick was used to hammer the intended piece into long splinters. Only one end of the stick was beaten with the maul, as the unbeaten part of the stick would be the handle.

2) A space was left open between the splinters of wood and the handle, then the handle just above the space was also beaten. The splinters thus formed were turned down over the lower splinters and all tied together with a rawhide thong, making a full broom.

Our brooms have many meanings besides keeping our floors in order. We use them as a signal to tell a person we are not at home when the broom is across the door. When the broom is just standing on the door frame, then it means "Come in, we will be right back." Sometimes there is no broom near the door or across the door; this leaves a question in the caller's mind, because the house is empty and the person has gone away on many errands.

To this day our people have never used the lock system or the police system, because everyone knows each other and we know that the contents of our houses are the same. We do not have more than the other fellow. We have no man-made riches, as the only rich people among us are the ones who have true and good friends.

Splint Brooms

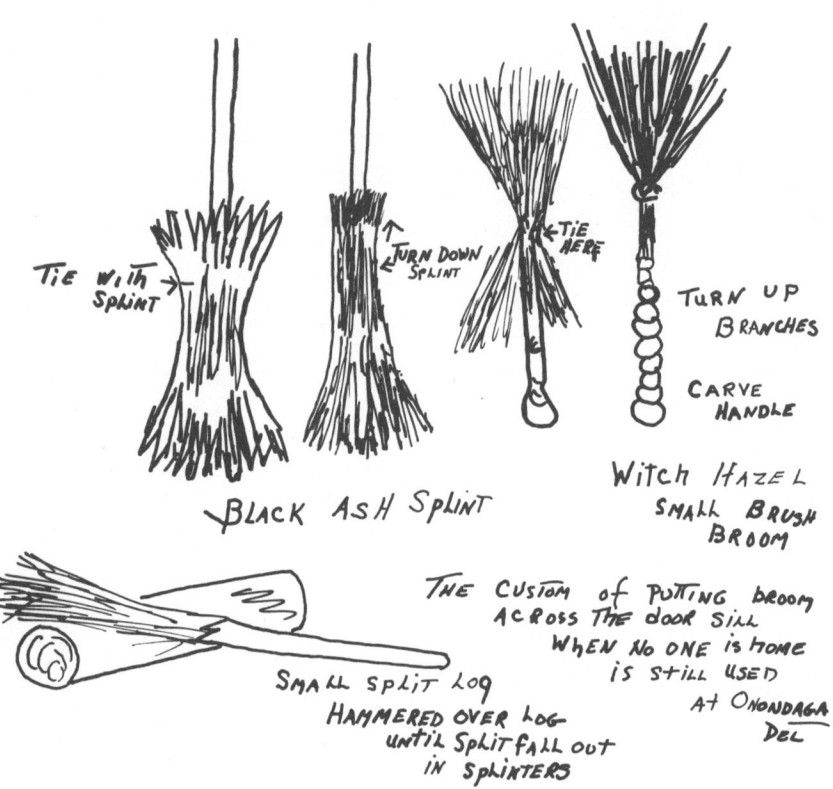

Pipes

The pipe is common to all Indian people.* In the old days to make smoke was to pray. Our people never did this without reason. Tobacco was always offered to the Unknown Quantity because in the Unknown Quantity my people found thanksgiving for things bestowed. They knew these blessings came from one greater than the human mind could ever be. As incense is burned in churches today, our people raised the smoke of the pipe to the four winds.

The pipe, to all Indian people, was supposed to be a living altar, with a head and body like a human being. The handle of the pipe symbolized the human spine. The bowl of the pipe the head - the soul of the pipe. The piece that joins the handle to the pipe is the breath of the pipe.

To offer the pipe was to offer communion. It was to establish a relationship of peace between friends and enemies alike. The pipe was smoked by the principal men of the nations to seal a friendship. Thus came the term ''peace pipe,'' although we used the pipe in other ceremonies, too.

When our people got together, regardless of whether they were chiefs or not, a pipe was passed

*In prehistoric times some North American Indian peoples did not use pipes or tobacco. —Editors' note.

around to symbolize that the group was joined together to concentrate on the problem before them. The pipe signified meditation. We believe all life is a circle, so that when a pipe was passed around and returned to the leader, it meant that each one was thinking on the problem. If all the people at the Council got up or if no one spoke, it signified that each one was still meditating and no one was yet ready to discuss the problem. They would remain until the situation was carefully thought out and finally discussed.

In the old days no young man was allowed to use the tobacco in this form (smoked in a pipe) until he had become an accomplished adult. By this we mean, until he had done something for his family and community that was constructive. When this had been accomplished, the honor went to the family, not to the individual.

A ceremony in which the pipe still has deep meaning is the Condolence Service. This ceremony is actually a eulogy, a recitation of all the things that have passed down to our people through the generations. Now, instead of each person making his own pipe, the Council buys them. The little individual pipes are passed out after the greeting. We know this is going to happen, so we automatically bring tobacco with us. The pipes, individually received, are marked for that particular occasion and kept as mementos.

At the Condolence Service the pipe represents meditation given to the departed chiefs and meditation on the candidate being judged and accepted as the new chief. Among our people this service gives a good feeling of being close to the Unknown.

CLAY PIPES

The Iroquois were noted for their clay pipes. Usually they used the clay found in the clay banks in the area in which they lived. This clay is a grayish color with a lot of dirt in it.

Sometimes bowls were attached to wooden stems which were elaborately decorated. The adornment might be hand carving on the stem or bird feathers or animal fur.

Our people frequently put effigies on the bowl. Many times it was the clan symbol. Non-Indians have had the idea that these effigies were something we worshipped. We did not.

Pipes

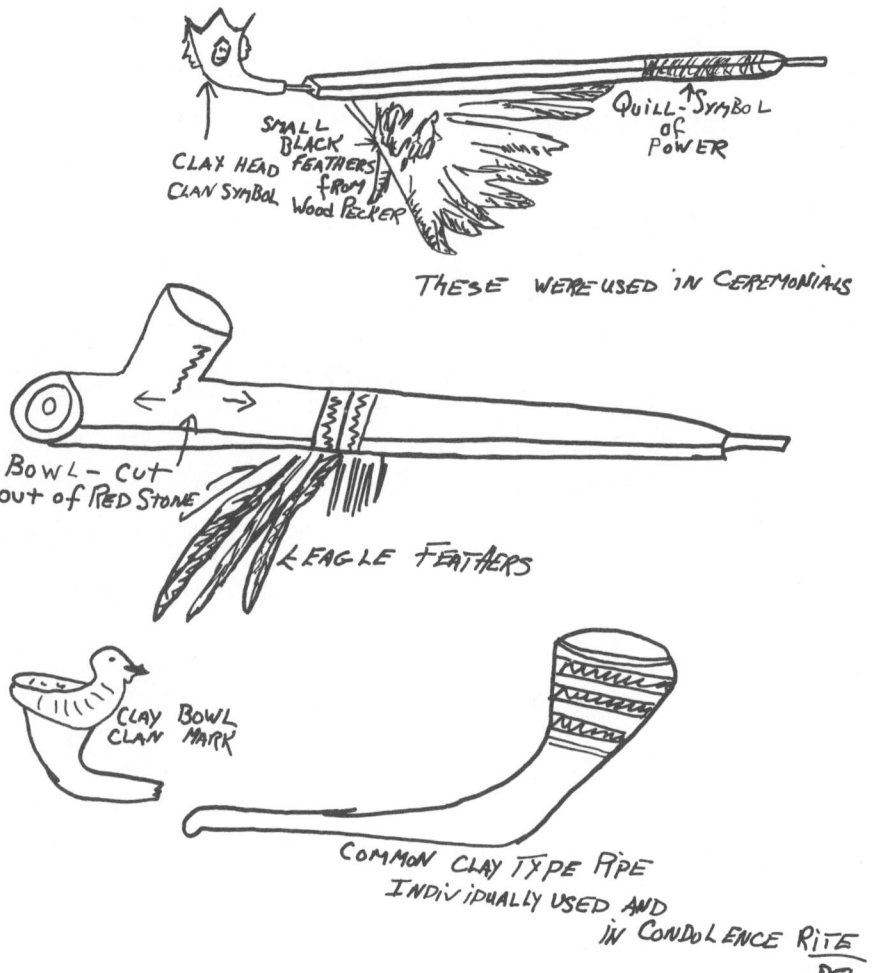

Bark Crafts

The Iroquois people used more bark crafts than any other. Without bark crafts we would not have had housekeeping utensils. At times historians have called these items "bark baskets" but to us they were bark containers. We used the containers to boil water, for mixing bowls (especially for mixing breads), as soup containers and as individual bowls -- any kind of utility container.

Some historians have made it appear that the Indians ate from a common pot. We had huge containers, as restaurants now do, for quantity cooking when large numbers gathered together, but we did not individually "dip into the pot." We would use a bark ladle, remove a portion to our individual bark bowl and eat with our individual spoons. This is why bark was such a big craft - we needed many containers and accessories from the bark.

Our people would obtain the bark during the time from the first or middle of May until the third week in June. During this period one can be fairly sure the tree will heal; at any other time the process is forced and the tree may be destroyed. Also, at this time no staining is liable to occur. Any other time the bark is apt to stain.

We would mark off the bark on a living tree, taking

only enough to make one article per tree. The wood for the containers and ladles was primarily elm bark. The rims of the containers were hickory, and the "thread" to sew them together was the inner bark, that portion between the outer bark and the tree itself. We used hickory for the rims because it can be molded by hand and does not have to be soaked in water to be bent. To our people bark containers were clean utensils for the preparation of food.

The Indians found that the elm bark acts like a lath so that they could coat the outside with clay or mud. Then they could put the container right on the coals of the fire, and the container could be used for cooking or boiling. Sometimes a top was fashioned for the cooking container. After the container had been used with the mud or clay coating, the protective coating could either be washed off so the container could be used for other purposes or the mud or clay could be repacked, and the container was again ready for cooking.

Another wood and bark that was important was the smooth bark hickory. Using the same process as described for elm, we could peel the hickory in oblong sheets. Again, we would only take one piece from a tree. Our people never made crafts by the dozens per day; we might make as many as three - one for us, one for a friend and one for reserve.

Hickory bark was used for rattles. We would take a strip of hickory, measure it to its midpoint and bend it over. This has to be done while it is green, almost immediately after it has been cut. The hickory will make its own shape. The rattle handles were made from a piece of hickory limb, with the rest of the limb frequently being used as rims for bark containers, and sometimes there would be enough to make a ladle. We wasted nothing. Corn or beans were used to make the noise inside the rattle. This type of bark rattle was used as a chant stopper in the ceremonials.

Hickory wood is one of the most versatile of the woods we used. Hickory is knot free, straight-grained. We used it for handles and rims for utensils, handles for rattles and canes, for snow snakes and lacrosse sticks.

Black ash was also important to us in our bark/wood crafts. Black ash splints for baskets were cut in the winter because the black ash is a swamp tree. To get to it we waited until the swamps froze. Also, the frost line would dry out the fiber enough so that the ash could be cut and pounded into strips. The rest of the year the trees were difficult to get to and the swamp kept the fibers too moist to do craft.

We would cut a tree, bring it home and cut it into four-foot to five-foot lengths. These pieces were pounded with a dull instrument at about six-inch intervals the first time around. The second time we would hit in between the first marks. We would keep rolling the piece around until the fiber loosened and came off at the end. If gotten at the right time, the ash will come off in strips. These strips are thin but not thin enough to be used for baskets. We would then roll the strips, place them in water until the craftsman was ready to make baskets.

When ready, the strips are dried. Using a scraper we would separate each strip layer by layer. This gives pliable, long strips we call splints. The first strips may not be as thin as those of the inner layers, so we would use them for the bottom. This black ash splint is strong, pliable, the ends can be rolled and almost any shaped basket can be made from it.

The core of the black ash, left after the splinting, was put to use. Sometimes it was used for carving or whatever utility could be imagined for it.

Our baskets were made of various sizes, depending on what we intended to use them for. We made some large enough to carry or store potatoes or other heavy produce.

Basswood, important to the carving of the masks, is discussed in the section on masks.

The trees were important in our lives. As children we learned not to abuse these special gifts that gave so much to us.

BARK LADLE

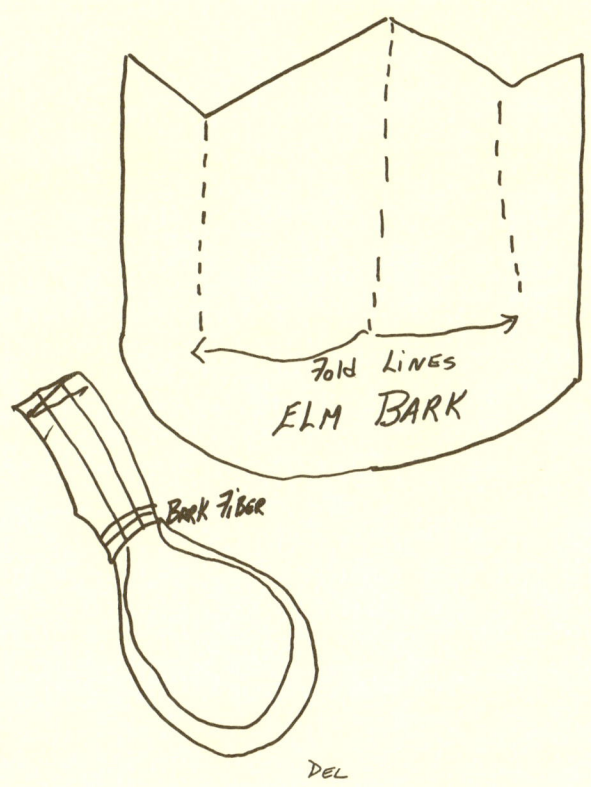

Rattles

The bark rattle is made at a certain time of the year, like May until the end of June. The bark rattle is used in nearly all our ceremonies.

To make a bark rattle, a piece of bark is taken from a young tree, as the bark is used better when it is thin; and it must be green. After stripping the bark from a tree we then immediately make the pattern of our rattle. We let the bark take its own position; being pliable, the bark will roll up in its original position. Then we take a small piece of wood to use as a plug to close the one opening. We take it home and hang to let dry. In this process the edges of the bark curl up around the plug and tighten, so it forms its own tie. Before this takes place, we put corn or beans inside this rattle. We are always careful not to make too many cuts from the young trees - one piece in one section of the woods.

We make other kinds of rattles from gourds, horns and turtle shells, but these are special ones just for the special services of our people.

The gourd rattle is used when people are ill, to notify the family. The turtle shell is used in the midyear services.* The horn rattle is used in all

---

*The turtle shell rattle also plays an important role in the False Face curing ceremony as well as in longhouse political meetings. — Editors' note.

services in social events. For the reason that the horn rattle is used universally among all my people, they have made many of them. They are stored in the longhouse. Anyone taking part in the ceremonies uses these rattles.

BARK RATTLES

PATTERN #I

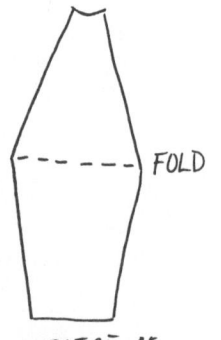

1. 1 PIECE OF BARK, CUT INTO THIS SHAPE & FOLD (NOTE 1 HALF IS WIDER)

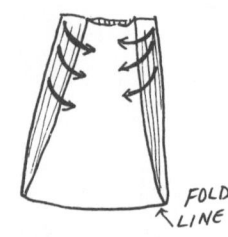

2. FOLD IN HALF, FOLD EDGES OF WIDER HALF OVER

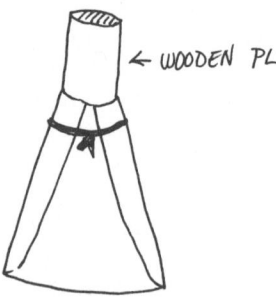

3. INSERT WOODEN PLUG, TIE UNTIL DRY

PATTERN #II

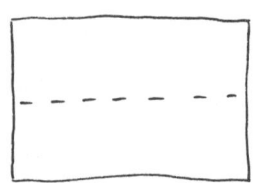

1. FOLD BARK IN HALF LENGTHWISE

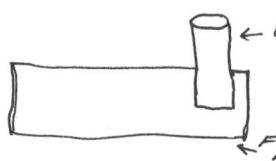

2. LAY PLUG ON FOLDED BARK & ROLL BARK AROUND PLUG

3. TIE & ALLOW TO DRY

WHEN DRY, REMOVE PLUGS, INSERT PEBBLES OR SEEDS (CORN, BEANS), & FINALLY INSERT A WOODEN HANDLE.

PRUCHNIK

HORN RATTLE

HORN PIECE

HOLES FOR PLUGS

CUT SECTION FROM COW HORN

CUT 2 PIECES OF WOOD TO FIT EACH END OF HORN

HOLE FOR PLUG

ONE PIECE OF WOOD

WOODEN PLUGS

INSERT PLUGS

FINISHED PRODUCT

HANDLE

JEAN PRUCHNIK

Cradleboard

Guy - hon - sach

Cradleboards were an important craft because of the family history they told and because it meant that the mother and child could be together. One can read a personal history in each cradleboard. In the art of the cradleboard the Iroquois could tell who he was and where he belonged -- an important factor to the Indian.

The Iroquois family was a close-knit unit. The children were and are looked on as the flower of family life, the seeds of the family's future. Propped in the fields or swinging gently from a tree branch, the child and the mother could watch each other, and when the time came, the cradleboard told the child his family history.

Guy - hon - sach is the Onondaga designation for the board because the jack-in-the-pulpit is the nearest similarity in nature to the baby in a cradleboard. *Guy - hon - sach* means the long hollow or a hollow straight up like a tube. The child fills the hollow, with the protective flap about his head, the silhouette resembles the jack-in-the-pulpit.

Families traced their history on the back of the board. Near the bottom of the board was a clan and/or nation symbol.¶ A short line with crossing lines through it could be symbolic of a feather denoting a partridge, a child of a Mohawk family. A pine tree signified the Onondaga.* The families were always careful to identify themselves in this fashion.

Usually in the middle or near the middle was an ornamental line. From this main stem would be other lines going off either side like branches of a tree. These branches had likenesses of flowers on them, which represented the number of daughters in that particular group. On the same plane but the opposite side of the stem would be another line with representations of fruit. These indicated the number of sons in that generation. Thus, looking at each plane a family could trace back the number of generations and the number of children - sons and daughters - in each.

Somewhere, usually near the top, might be the symbol of the eagle. Indian legend tells that the eagle was all-powerful and watched over all. With this ability and concern, the eagle was the medium for conveying prayers to the Creator. It symbolizes respect for the unknown.

¶Del's clan symbol is the snipe, and the pine tree is the nation symbol. — Editors' note.
*The Iroquois comprise six nations: Onondaga, Mohawk, Cayuga, Oneida, Seneca and later, the Tuscarora. Del mentions five nations in her chapter on costumes. — Editors' note.

These designs were cut into the wood. The Indians engraved with sharp stones or the ends of bone and, later, with metal tools. Cradleboards were made primarily from basswood, though other soft woods were used. The reeds across the top were hickory. These extended beyond the back of the board so that the baby could be propped up at an angle rather than resting flat on the ground. Mothers could then see the child and the child, the mother.

Cradleboards were passed down to the eldest daughter, who then continued keeping the family record. If there were other daughters, they started their own family records.*

---

*As the eldest daughter of her family, Del kept her family cradleboard; she generously donated it to the AIAI. — Editors' note.

CRADLE BOARD

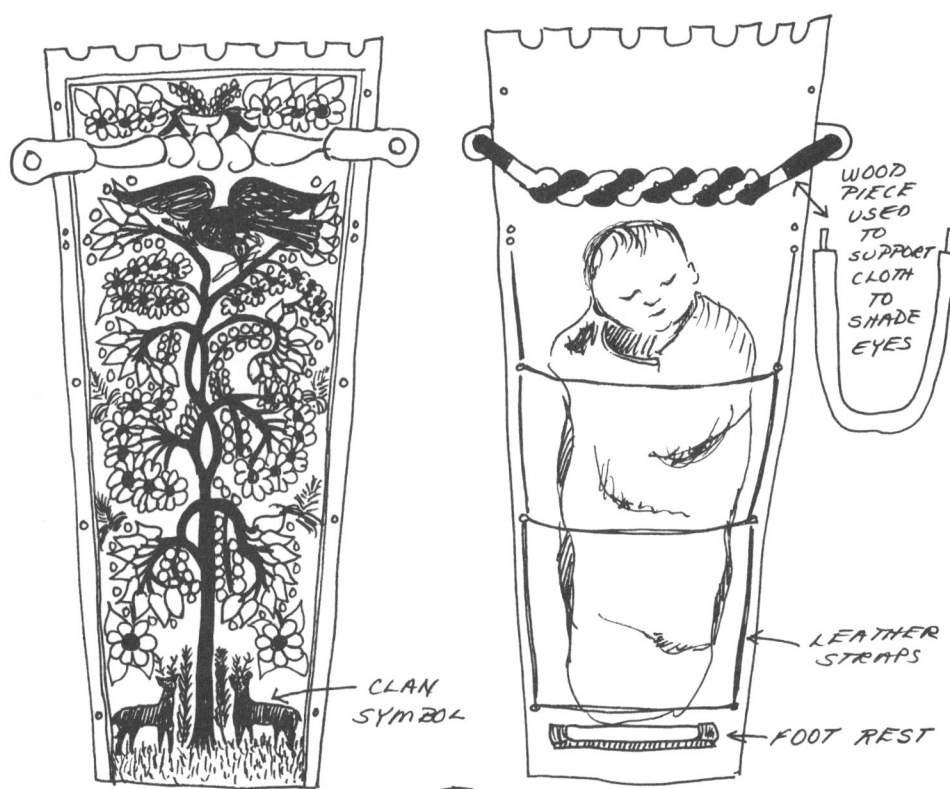

CLAN SYMBOL

WOOD PIECE USED TO SUPPORT CLOTH TO SHADE EYES

LEATHER STRAPS

FOOT REST

BACK OF BOARD HAS FAMILY HISTORY CARVED OUT- FRUIT FOR BOYS, FLOWERS FOR GIRLS

PRUCHNIK

JACK-IN-THE-PULPIT IS THE SAME ONONDAGA INDIAN NAME FOR CRADLE

GUY-HON-SACH
BUNDLED BOX — BENT SAPLING

Costumes of the Iroquois People

Costumes* of the Iroquois people were made of animal skins until the coming of the first white explorers and traders. At that time each separate tribe of the Iroquois Confederacy -- Mohawks, Oneidas, Onondagas, Cayugas and Senecas -- exchanged and traded whole skins for cloth and began to make their garments from this material. They found cloth to have the advantages of being easier to keep clean, easier to wash and easier to work with.

Earliest evidence shows that broadcloth was brought in by the English and French about 1537. With the coming of Champlain in 1607 cloth became more generally available to all of the Eastern Woodland Indians. As cotton materials became more plentiful, silk and velvet were also introduced. These were used for decoration of the broadcloth garments.

Cloth became a very important trading item. So important that when treaties were made between the United States government and the individual tribes, the treaty frequently stipulated that a yearly grant of cloth would go to the tribe to meet one of the practical needs of the people. A treaty ratified in 1794 with the United States saw the Iroquois ceding large tracts of land in the Ohio Valley to the United States, and as

*Del used this word to mean clothing. —Editors' note.

part of this exchange the Iroquois were to be paid in bolts of cloth. As time passed the government of the United States ceased to fulfill its promise to give bolts of cloth. Today the Iroquois people receive a small amount of yardage per person per year. It has become tradition for each family to make their family costumes from the treaty grant cloth.

The federal government is now asking that the Iroquois accept money instead of cloth for the 1794 Treaty. This is asked to ease the bookkeeping in the federal office. The Iroquois people feel that this token payment in cloth represents an obligation on the part of the United State government to keep its word. If payment in money were accepted by the Iroquois, the words of the treaty would be broken.

The original costume of the Iroquois women consisted of animal skins wrapped around the body like a skirt. It overlapped left to right, much as the present-day wraparound skirt is made. Gradually leggings were added for warmth, moccasins for the protection of the feet. The overblouse or tunic was much like the present-day maternity dress.

Early cloth garments were made like the skin garments. Gradually the clothing became patterned after the European fashions, but native decorations were still used. These decorations were in the form of trimming and used native quills, beads and fringe.

The meaning of the designs are interpreted by their pattern and by the colors used. Three basic colors - red, white and black - have significance in all designs. These designs are all border designs and have full figures represented on them.

In the decoration of the skirt the sky outline was frequently used as a running design along the hem and ended with a tree design that was worked upward toward the waist. The tree design included curving branches outward signifying life. Sometimes a corner design of a small tree was worked in to signify light in the middle of earth.

The overblouse or tunic was the result of European influence. It was made to be a loose fitting garment, usually gathered at the waist by an outside belt. It had full sleeves and a ruffled (gathered) yoke. As a rule the whole garment was edged with white beadwork.

Leggings were made in bright red or dark blue cloth. They opened in the front and were heavily beaded on each side of the opening. It was traditional to edge the leggings with beadwork around the bottom.

Headbands worn by the women had the same significance that a wedding band has in European society. A single woman wore a beaded headband with a feather fastened on one side of her head. A married woman wore the headband, also, but the feather was fastened on the back of her head.

The costumes described are seldom seen any more because they are generally used only in the religious ceremonies or services.

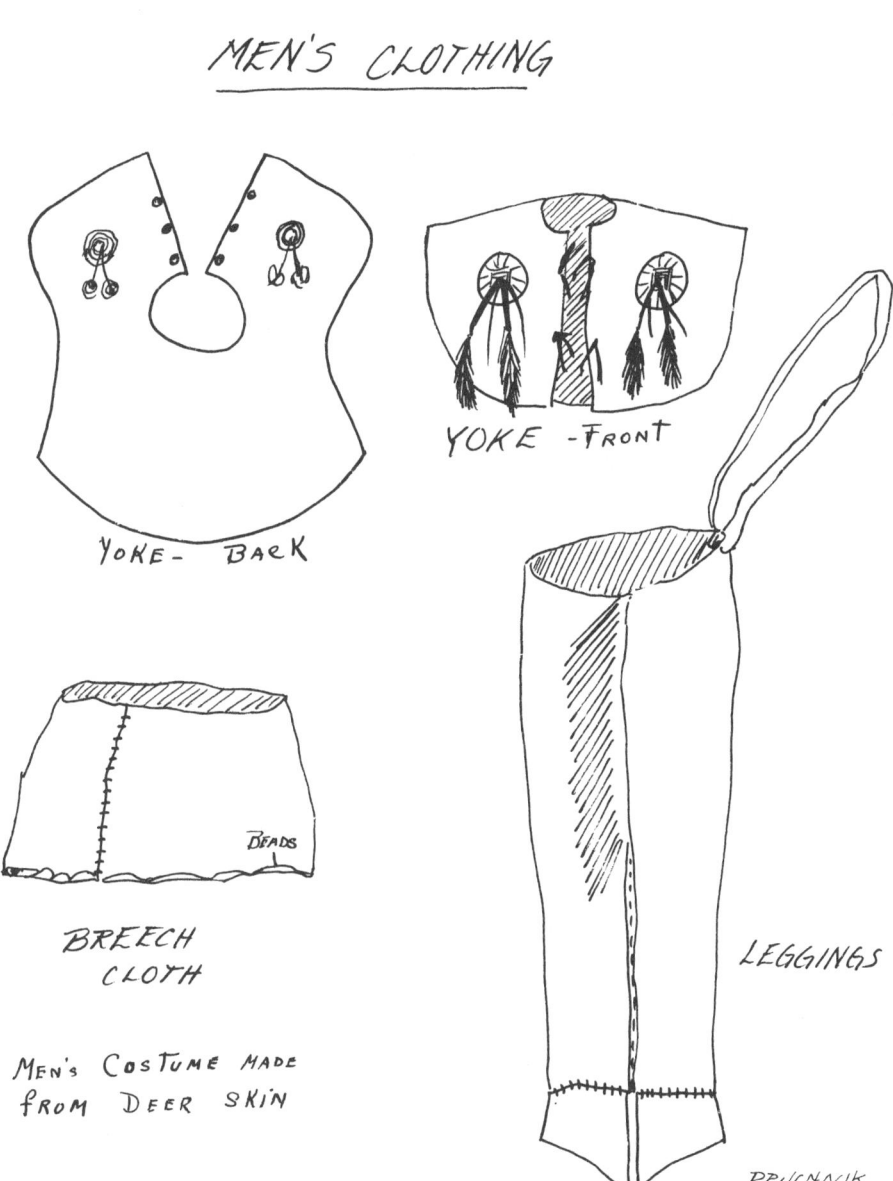

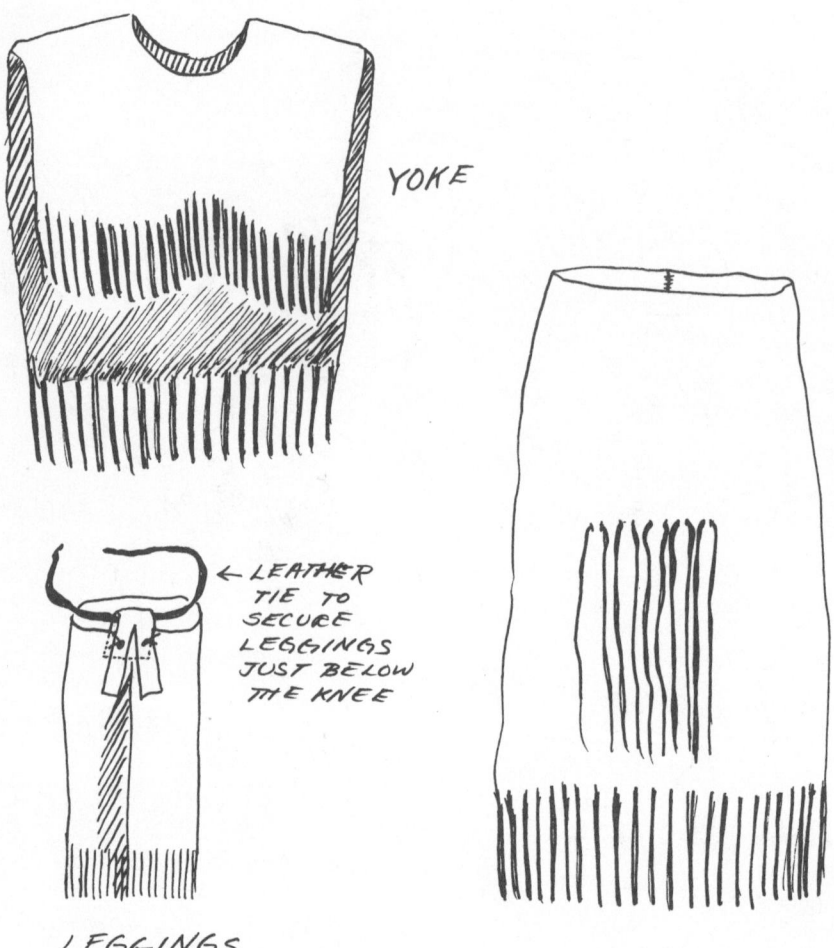

MOCCASINS

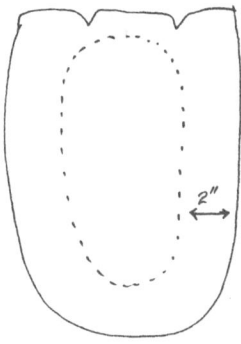

1. CUT LEATHER ABOUT 2 INCHES MORE THAN OUTLINE OF FOOT.

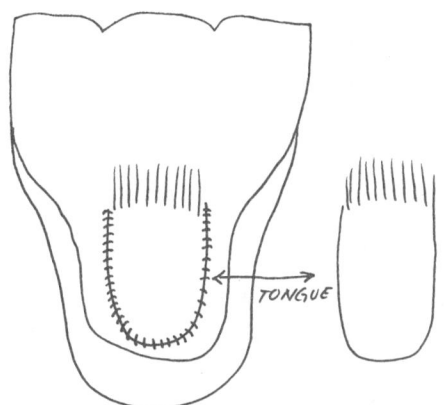

2. CUT TONGUE ABOUT 1/3 SIZE OF UPPER FOOT DESIGN

3. PUCKER THE TONGUE TO FIT SIZE OF ACTUAL FOOT DESIGN

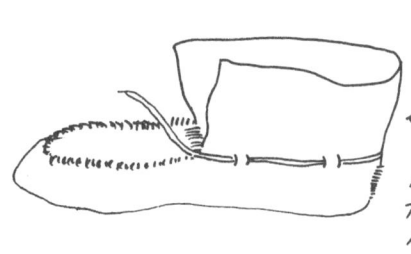

← TOP FLAP THIS CAN BE 1 PIECE OR A PIECE ADDED AS A CUFF

4. SEW HEEL

PRUCHNIK

Iroquois Basket Cap

Gus-t-weh

The form was made of four narrow splints bound together with a fifth splint interwoven diagonally and down. This not only held the headband together but served as decoration for the band. Two splints were fastened together at right angles and their ends were shoved between the splints of the basket cap.

A basswood wooden block was then whittled down at one end to serve as a plume holder. A wooden pin was cut to fit inside with a wide base so that it could not be pulled through the opening. When a circular piece of leather with four tie strings was pulled over the plume holder and fastened to the top of the cap, it held the block firmly in place.

The end of a feather's quill was snipped off and the feather pushed down over the pin into the plume holder. Split feathers were also pushed down into the holder, completing the decoration. Sometimes the entire frame was covered with velvet or skin, or could be worn with just the frame.

BASKET CAP

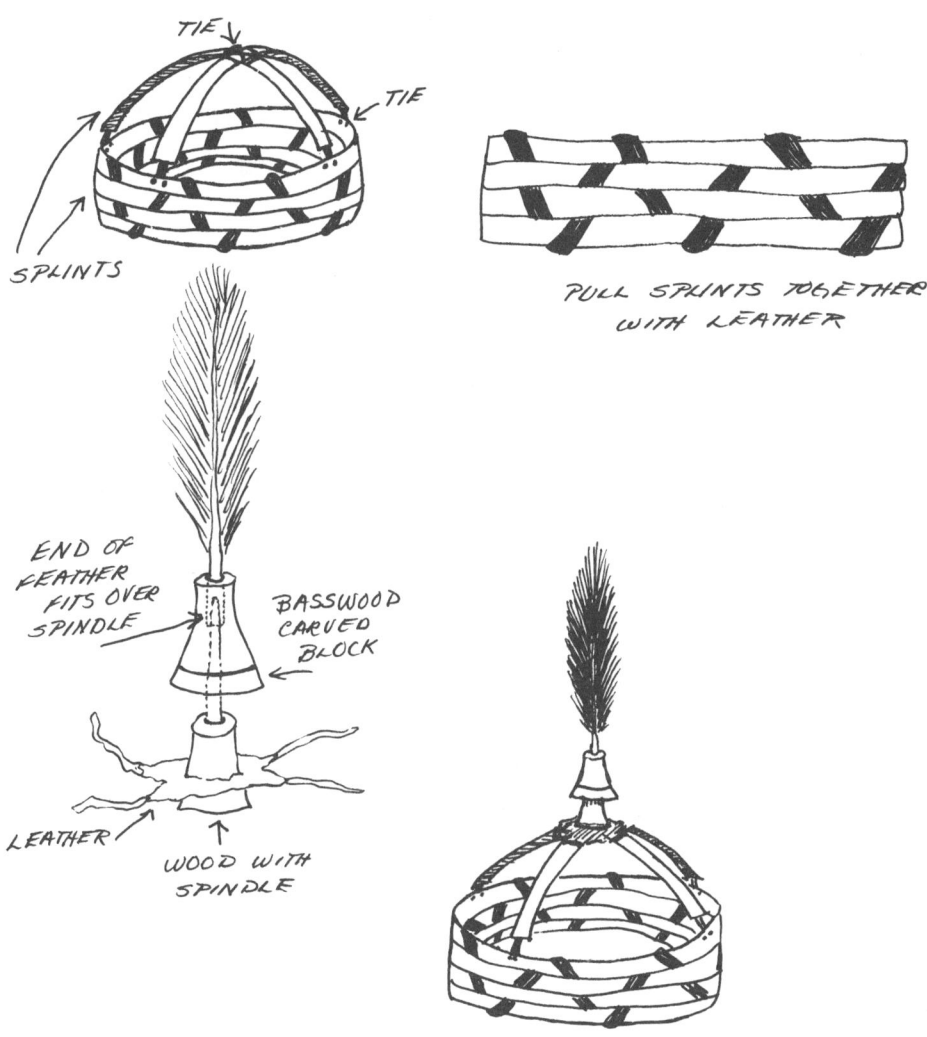

PRUCHNIK

Masks

The mask carver of my people is a man who is an artist in his own right. True mask carvers not only understand their material and have the skills to develop it but also have a knowledge, understanding and respect for the meaning and use of the mask.

Basically there are eight masks that have the greatest significance in our circle of life. The ceremonial masks are not used by everyone. Only those who have won the respect of the people participate in the services using the mask.

Many non-Indians have regarded the masks with curiosity and misunderstanding. They have called the masks grotesque, magical—to my people they are symbols, reminders of lessons important to the individual's life circle. The mask makes the person wearing it impersonal, so when we see the mask in the ceremony we think only of the lesson the mask represents.

As an example, the most frequently seen mask in books and museums is the one the non-Indian calls "Crooked Face." To us this mask represents the greed and conceit, the selfishness and unreliability in man and reminds us to discipline these qualities within ourselves.

According to our lesson, the **Creator** came to earth

to survey his creation. As the Creator walked along, man came to his side and walked with him. The Creator asked man if there was anything that could be added for the comfort of man or if there was anything more man needed. In his humble way the Creator walked and talked with man. Man, however, did not recognize his companion and decided to show off his authority and power. Man refuted the Creator's words and told Creator that he, man, had made all that was there. The more he talked, the more man boasted.

The Creator was disturbed by man's gloating, for this was not the way he intended man to be. Creator decided to teach man a lesson, so he challenged man to move a mountain that was before them. They agreed that whoever could move the mountain the farthest would prove that that one was the Creator. Man agreed to the challenge, but wanted his challenger to go first.

The Creator knew that man could not be trusted, even though man had promised to turn his back and not look when his challenger took his turn at moving the mountain. When the Creator was moving the mountain, man did look to see how his opponent was doing it. As man turned to look, the mountain came rushing by, crushing man's face and distorting it.

In our services the wearer of this mask provides an impersonal reminder that we must be humble and honorable in our dealings with others and ourselves. The stories symbolized by our masks could be compared to the parables of the Christian Bible.

Another example is the Grandfather Mask. This mask is typical of the Onondaga Nation because Onondaga, more than any other group, has retained the things from the past. The Grandfather Mask is one of our largest. Non-Indians frequently call it gruesome; it is not. This mask has to have large features, and because the mask carver knows the meaning, he carves it in this fashion.

The grandfather, in the family of the American Indian, has passed through much of life's circle. He is wisdom. Grandfather teaches boys how to hunt, he teaches conservation; he has taught his grandchildren the legends and their lessons, and now he sits. He sits and calls his chants from his drum. He is ready to watch what happens. Grandfather is there to console and to be consulted. He sits with his wisdom—and shares it when asked. Grandfather is a bridge from past to present.

During our services, when the Grandfather Mask appears it symbolizes the presence of wisdom. It causes us to think about our lives, what we need to be counseled about, the need to think wisely before we act. Again, without preaching at us, all we need to see is the mask and we remember our lesson.

The Spoon-mouth Mask has been greatly romanticized by the non-Indian. They say it is a curing mask, that we believe this mask has potency to cure the ill. Our people are not willing to correct someone else's mistakes or misinterpretations. If others want to romanticize it, it is all right with us. We know the meaning of the symbol, and that is what is important.

Our people have always known about herbs and medicines. We frequently shared this knowledge with the early pioneers. We have particular people who are very knowledgeable about these plants and their uses. They were our doctors. The non-Indian romanticized them by calling them "medicine men." Our people also have prayers for the healing process, but so do other religious groups. The Indian also recognizes that outdoor life makes bodies strong and that the body needs to be cared for.

The Spoon-mouth Mask reminds us to maintain health and to respect our bodies. Recognizing life as a circle, and that we return "to ashes," we use "Spoon-mouth" to remind us of these things and to give thanks when someone regains health. During the midyear ceremonies, the wearer of the "Spoon-mouth" blows ashes in the blessing of each home, much as Christianity uses ashes in its blessings and rites.

One of the lesser known masks is that of the "Stone

Giant." This mask represents one of the oldest stories, or lessons, of our people. When the Stone Giant Mask is used, it is to remind the young people about conservation.

Many, many years ago there were people called the Stone Giants. They lived in caves and their bodies were encased in a flint-like crust. Their stamping grounds were Onondaga Hill and the caves. These people wanted to eliminate the customs and ways of my people and thus dominate the group now known as the Iroquois. They were greatly feared by the Iroquois people.

Our people noticed that there was a certain time of the year when the Stone Giants would invade the villages of the Onondagas. . . when our people were joined together to celebrate the festivals of thanks, especially the corn festival and the festival of the harvest. After becoming aware of this, our people decided to withhold the Thanksgiving prayer services until the invasions stopped.

We found there was one person who could help us. He had the welfare of my people in his hands. We call him the "Holder of Heaven." He is believed to have sent a go-between, a person who understood our people and mastered the traits of the Stone Giants. Gradually, he was able to decoy the Stone Giants into invading by small groups and was able to do away with them. However, one escaped, going to the mountains of the Alleghenies.

One day one of our hunters took shelter from a thunderstorm in a cave. He heard a voice telling him that he was invading the property of the Stone Giants. Our hunter looked deep into the cave but saw nothing; he could only hear the voice. The voice told him that in order to have his life spared, the hunter must do what the voice told him. Our hunter agreed.

The Stone Giant said that he had been able to escape because he had promised to do good things for the Onondagas. The Stone Giant could not go among them. Therefore, the Stone Giant required the hunter to go among his own people and teach them the lessons the Stone Giant was going to give to the hunter.

They sat together, the hunter and the voice of the Stone Giant. The hunter learned that he must live to do only good, to go among his people teaching. . . that each living thing has an individual spirit of its own; that the different kinds of woods were used for different things; that there must always be new plants to replace the plants used; that one took no more than one needed; that humans should understand they were just one part of all life and that they would always have obstacles to overcome; that without a goal in life, the human portion of the living things would become restless.

The hunter listened for a long time, learning about the nature of life, the woods, the plants, the humans—and their survival in harmony. When the Stone Giant finished the hunter realized that he was sitting near a basswood tree. The tree told him that whenever he carved on basswood, he must offer a prayer of thanks through the medium of tobacco. Then a nearby hickory spoke up and told him the time of year to take the hickory bark, and so it went with the woods and plants.

Thus it is said that the Stone Giant taught us conservation. When we see this mask we honor it for it is the first mask. It is our reminder of conservation of all the elements making up the earth and appreciation of them.

As previously indicated, the mask and its use has been most misunderstood. Non-Indians, particularly the settlers, have not recognized that the Indians have cultures. There were few who befriended Indians on the basis of accepting their culture or wanting to truly understand. Gradually, non-Indians looked on Indians as curiosities: they wanted to bring cameras, to be amused—even in the area of religion. Our religion is sacred to us. Finally, our Council had to decree that no non-Indian could view the religious ceremonies. Other religious groups do not like to be laughed at. . .

they hold up a cross or a star, they burn incense, they use ashes. Why do people think the Indian is a funny curiosity because he has masks and tobacco as symbols of life's lessons? Secret masked societies? Not secret to the Indian.

There are times masks are used for social occasions. The young boys make cloth masks with long noses, just like a clown, covering his face. This gives the youngsters a chance, especially the shy ones, to show how well they have learned the social dances. Because the masks make them "unknown" or impersonal to the viewers, the child is not self-conscious. They learn to participate equally, that each has a contribution to make to the whole. This is a feature of the twenty-eight day midyear ceremony.

WOODEN MASKS

Mask carving is blocked out on a living basswood tree. There are eight basic masks representing eight different "parables," which teach us a lesson. The mask is cut in high relief. Masks started and completed in the morning are painted red; masks completed in the afternoon are painted black. Horsehair is sometimes added to the mask, but this is not characteristic of the very early masks.

CROOKED FACE

Spoon Mouth

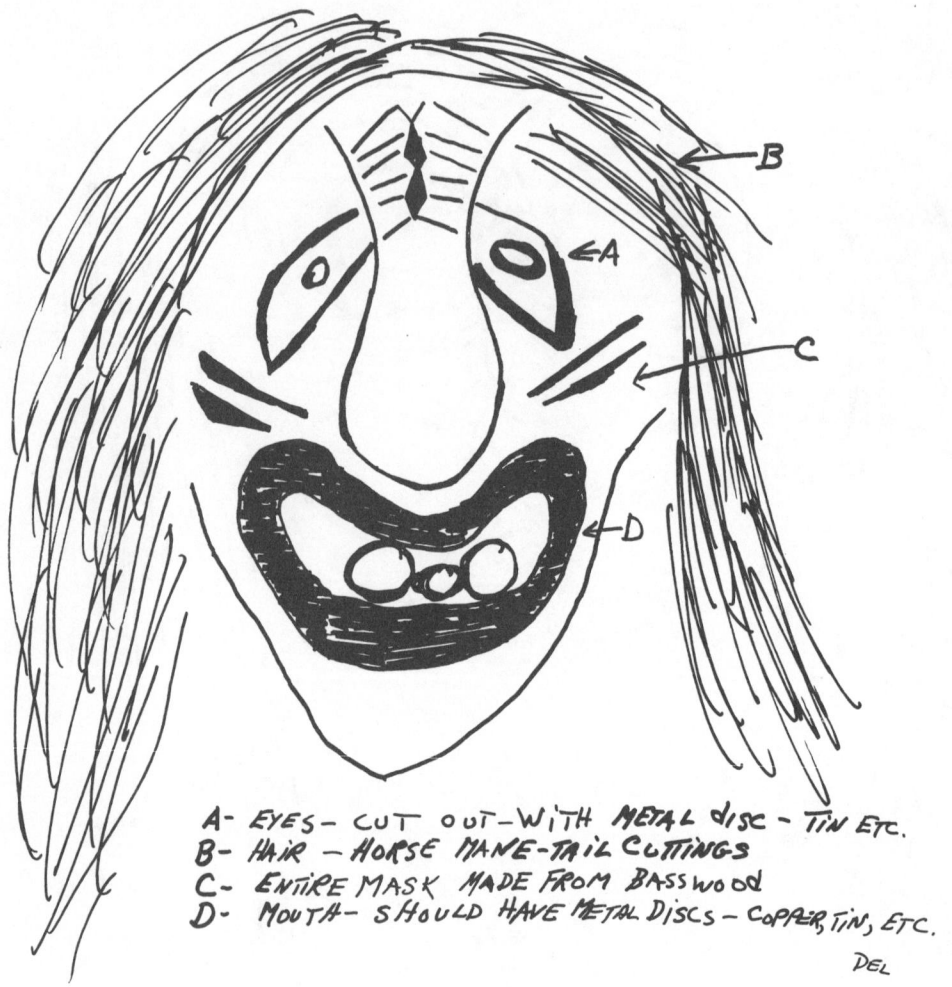

A - EYES - CUT OUT - WITH METAL disc - TIN ETC.
B - HAIR - HORSE MANE - TAIL CUTTINGS
C - ENTIRE MASK MADE FROM BASSWOOD
D - MOUTH - SHOULD HAVE METAL DISCS - COPPER, TIN, ETC.

DEL

Stone Giant Mask

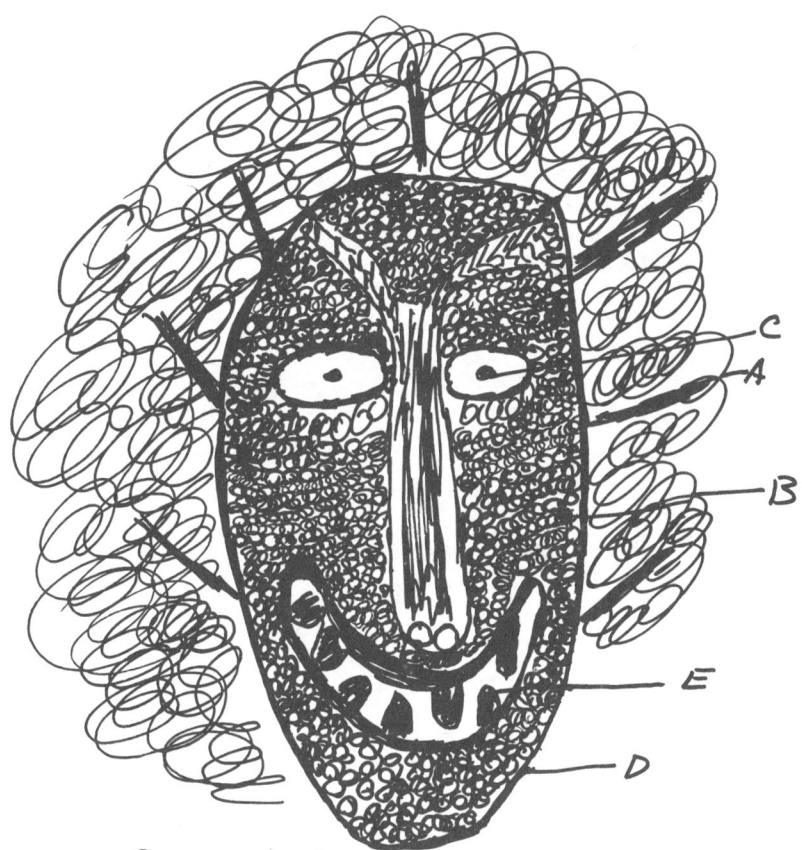

A - Basswood Wood Fiber
B - Stone Pebbles over Pitch (many times hemlock)
C - Eye Holes Stone Embedded
D - Basswood
E - Teeth - Shaped from Stone Embedded

*Del instructing basketmaking at the
American Indian Archaeological Institute*

Adelphena Logan

An Onondaga Iroquois, Del was a direct descendant of Logan, chief of the Cayuga Iroquois. She was born on the Cattaraugus-Seneca Indian Reservation on June 9, 1912, and died at the Onondaga Reservation on July 31, 1978.

Del's life was full.

Del was educated at Alfred, Syracuse and Columbia Universities.

Del was Director of Arts and Crafts for the Syracuse Parks and Recreation Department for more than thirty years.

Del was Assistant Indian Planning Director for the Cayuga County Museum.

Del was Assistant Director of the Owasco Restored Indian Village and Museum in Auburn, New York.

Del was an instructor for the Rochester Museum of Arts and Sciences.

Del was a trustee or board member of:
- Cayuga County Museum (twenty-one years)
- American Indian Archaeological Institute (six years)
- Channel 24 Educational Television, Syracuse, New York
- The President's twelve-member Commission on Indian Awareness as the Woodland Indian Representative
- New York State Board of Indian Achievement on State Relations with Indians.

Del was a member of:
- Alpha Phi Sorority, an educational sorority
- The Smithsonian Institution
- New York State Authors' Group, Syracuse Chapter
- Delta Kappa Gamma, a women's educational honorary society
- Cayuga County Museum Association
- Onondaga Historical Association.

Del was a consultant informally to all who were privileged to know her, and formally to:
- Smithsonian Institution's Board of Indian Arts and Crafts
- American Indian Archaeological Institute
- Rochester Museum of Arts and Sciences (on Iroquois crafts for ten years)
- Cayuga County Museum (twenty-one years)
- Auburn Community College (on Iroquois history)
- Syracuse Folk Arts of the Cultural Resources Council (on Iroquois lore).

Del was awarded the Cornplanter Medal from the Cayuga County Historical Society for service to and knowledge of Iroquois Indians.

Del was the first person to receive the Burl Ives Award on Indian lore for Eastern Indians **twice**.

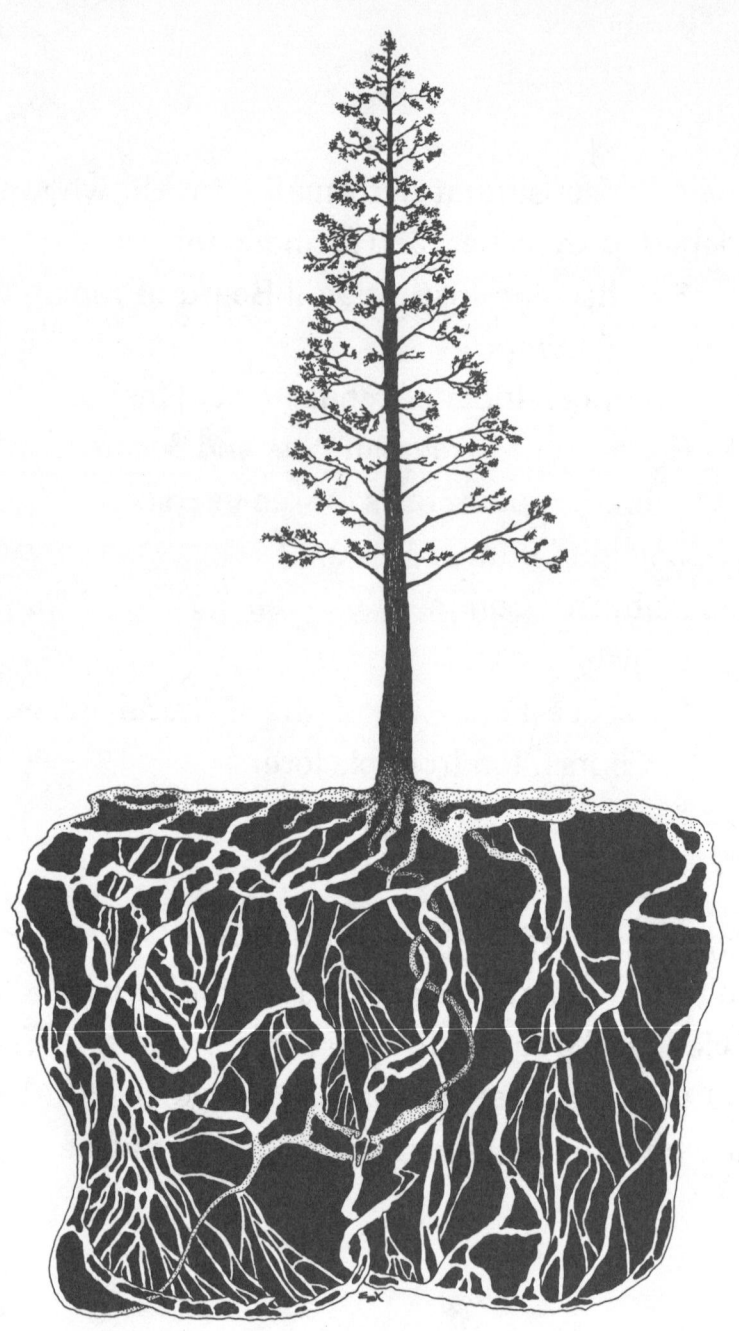

The White Pine symbolizes the Iroquois League reaching high into the sky, its white roots reaching to the four winds. It offers shelter and protection to any man or nation, for this is the Law of the Great Peace.

ONONDAGA INDIAN PRAYER

O Great Creator
Whose voice I always listen for in the winds,
Hear me — I am small — part of you — I need wisdom.
Let me walk in your beauty,
Make my hands respect the things you have made,
Keep my ears ever sharp for your voice,
Help me to travel a Path of Wisdom,
      so I may understand all people.
I seek knowledge — not to be greater than my brother,
But to learn to share a greater understanding.
Make me always helpful and ready to come to all
Earthly causes with clean hands and clean thoughts.
Amen.

Del opened and closed AIAI gatherings with this prayer.
Editors' Note.

ACKNOWLEDGEMENTS

All of us at the American Indian Archaeological Institute, who had the good fortune of knowing Del and learning from her, are honored to be able to contribute to this posthumous publication of **Memories of Sweet Grass**. Del's memories, which she so generously shared with us, and finally was persuaded to write down and illustrate, have become a part of our lives; we now leave them with you.

Editorial consultant: Joan Van Keuren

AIAI editorial consultants:

    Trudie Ray Lamb   Sharon Wirt
    Dave Richmond   Susan Payne

AIAI artistic contributors:

    Jean Pruchnik   Barrie Kavasch

11741